# I LOST $25 ATTEMPTING TO MAKE A PROFIT FROM THIS BOOK BY WORKING FROM HOME! AND YOU CAN TOO!

## By Michael Gross

Worker ID: A1AJ35NTQ1DARP

## Supporting Authors:

ELITE, REV, TURKOPTICON, MITSUKU, A1ODX4HG1VLAYC, A1YGSIQI52QT9L,
AG1FD1CXC2Y22, A1GRN111GB7MPR, A1OY5QALCRY3Z4, A26U4IKXMXT0ZA,
A3RBC5DVESRSEB, A17VXAMGTXV1FL, A1SMAPOIC2E7YH, A2VI55LKT5L4KB,
A3AMYG3X8AQJ0N, AGV6593PUKY0Q, AK5AFB4VLBCGK, ADAGUJNWMEPT6,
AD1ILDUXZHASF, A3ES4BXB8PJWTX, AQE6A9JJM7FZM, A2089GGBHBLVSQ,
A2UNSF09FWX9S8, A1N4P4XGQM7NXE, A2RVUSQQ0150J2,
A3JTMXHPNCUFNX, A3HJC6BU35CPE0, A5DSYVNGYLCA5, A17J1CE7N49Z9D,
A3MS21UJPMHLK0, A2X6K5T4P6GXTY, AKHO08K69B4Y4,
A1V1BWPEQX90X1, A2LZ9KG42SZ3I0, A2M3LVBUZLN8MO, AZZZYAYJQSDOJ,
ALDQRWYZ8KQ9A, A3EJI3R6ZE9Y4X, A29HS8UKNCMCQU, A1OK974KXKO6FJ,
AUR6U2RJAGUTF, A6QMYJ1FWU9QA, A11DOB7V9YBL4S, A3UITZ4R9EE75I,
AQK9RIOA9FURX, A8VAJKHA3AA7J, A23CTGXNDDW5LC, A3FPXLLF0B8CIC,
A2BLA8KJIAMXTW, A3PD06OTVDYTQN, AEY67OL8UKB, A2OZO0I3XX690K,
A2SFAW068VC8C6, A3V2XOIEVMYEBQ, A1NOGVJ7O47IOO, A2T50IRD435JRZ,
AJTAAGXRG14UA, A1XACRIZ51TBMY, A2I60HA5UXITYS, A2Z6Y7MS2ZNTC5,
A1GV0UZU0T2ORS, A68CSKRK4XJBX, A1JV64BL3WCK0G, A22I15PKMDDBU5,
A3U2JWLJ4IAPZ, A36VA1TSX3RYED, A12R2U6TBB3OOG

# Foreword

The new ability to telecommute, i.e. work remotely from home, is hailed because it's able to help anyone get their job done regardless of barriers like commute times or disability. That's an amazing thing, truly. By that logic, websites like Amazon Mechanical Turk are great because they give people more opportunities to make some side money without barriers, right? The emphasis really should be on "side money," because what these sites pay is abysmal in proportion to the hours devoted to them. So why are there so many workers on Mechanical Turk "turking" at this very moment?

Working from home is attractive because it seems to be immediate gratification for the intellectual and mechanical labor we engage in on a daily basis. If you were told you could be paid for every tweet you wrote, you'd jump on that, right? Obviously that's not what you actually do when you telecommute, but that is definitely the idyllic vision companies focused around the work-from-home model or the "share economy" enforce on their workers.

What isn't ever discussed is the isolation, or the sheer amount of hours necessary for a modicum of okay payment. It seems obvious, but unless you have things outside the job to see, the interior of your apartment, house, or storage unit that you're squatting in is all you're going to see while you work. The work that was so attractive because it was all about being self-driven and self-scheduled becomes maddening quickly because the only one you have to answer to and interact with is yourself. The stress becomes worsened when it becomes clearer that the pay received makes no sense. While visiting the subreddit for Mechanical Turk, I came across a conversation where a user was incredulous that another poster was taking 8 hours to earn $20 while turking. He reassured him that it was much simpler, emphasizing that it only takes him *4 to 6 hours* to get $20, the Turk maven that he is.

That being said, my approach to getting these workers closer to their $20 a day limit was to get them money by simply being humans. That is, by lying to me. By simply creatively lying to my questionnaires, these workers can find respite in my questions and really go hog wild and say whatever they please. From what I understand of the working process for Turk workers, constant grinding and replaying of HITs is the key to efficiently working, not unlike a video game that sucks your soul out in exchange for a sick outfit for your imaginary character. This project aims to reinsert some of that soul into the equation.

**WORKER ID**
A1ODX4HG1VLAYC

**What do you do when you are alone?**
I will run to the top of the house and says I am the happiest man in the field.

**Describe your last sexual encounter (use your own definition of "sexual encounter")**
I slapped my partner and enjoyed my drinks

**What was the last emotion you felt?**
I cried very happily when i got accident.

**A human walking in front of you drops a $20 bill and continues to walk. What do you do?**
I take down $20 and destroy it with fire lighter.

**Give me your abbreviated life story.**
I was born in Mars .At the age of 5,i arrived earth with my twin brother.I got doctorate degree at the age of 12.i run a business and my workers are under the age of 10.I have one of my house in Mars.I often traveled from Earth to Mars.

-$0.25

**WORKER ID**
A1YGSIQI52QT9L

**What do you do when you are alone?**
When I am alone I would like to read some book alongwith Internet surfing

**Describe your last sexual encounter (use your own definition of "sexual encounter")**
Sexual Encounter does not exist in my emotion

**What was the last emotion you felt?**
I am neutral right now because I have no any happy news

**A human walking in front of you drops a $20 bill and continues to walk. What do you do?**
I will not do special and I will ignore him

**Give me your abbreviated life story.**
I have no abbreviated life story right now

-$0.25

**WORKER ID**
A12R2U6TBB3OOG

**What do you do when you are alone?**
I usually will wait until I'm alone to work on my plans to rob the local credit union.

**Describe your last sexual encounter (use your own definition of "sexual encounter")**
I got stuck working late at the office last week. The new intern was there as well, she's still learning the ropes, so she's a bit slow at her job. Anyway, I offered her a ride home since it was late and raining and she would have to wait alone for the next bus. While I was driving, she started groping me and then stuck her hand in my pants. We pulled off into a parking lot and had sex in the back seat of my car.

**What was the last emotion you felt?**
I train my dog for agility competitions as a hobby. I took her to a regional competition this past weekend, and we won first place. That was the happiest felt in a long time.

**A human walking in front of you drops a $20 bill and continues to walk. What do you do?**
I would immediately step on it and hide it under my foot while I pretend to look at my phone. When I'm sure nobody has seen me with the money, I would bend down and act like I'm tying my shoe, then I'd snatch up the money and continue on my way.

**Give me your abbreviated life story.**
I grew up in Alaska. My parents run a hotel/restaurant near Denali National Park. Even though our town was pretty remote, I had a mostly normal upbringing. I moved to Chicago after high school and went to culinary school with the plan being that I would take over my family's restaurant sometime in the near future. That's where I'm at currently.

-$0.25

**WORKER ID**
A36VA1TSX3RYED

**What do you do when you are alone?**
I tell my half dozen cabana boys to leave the room because I'm never alone with these guys around. Okay so now that I'm really alone, I jump into my bathtub which is full of rice pudding and cherry sauce and watch the movie Rover Dangerfield nonstop for 23 and a half hours.

**Describe your last sexual encounter (use your own definition of "sexual encounter")**
Most of that is classified information. I don't think the government of Quaz'nar Ob would appreciate hearing about how I watched their equivalent of a prime minister snort space cocaine while in the nude off of my mahogany table.

**What was the last emotion you felt?**
Existential dread and doom. Ha, I'm kidding, I haven't felt emotions since they took my brain out of my old meat and bone suit and put it in this fancy plasteel body. I have no need for emotions anymore.

**A human walking in front of you drops a $20 bill and continues to walk. What do you do?**
What can I do? I am powerless as I watch the bill fall into the void, falling for an eternity, falling as I watch for an eternity. The world no longer exists. I no longer exist. The bill no longer exists. I begin to lose my mind. Then the bill hits the ground and so do I. I fold it into a paper airplane and throw it in the general direction of the person then turn 360 degrees and moonwalk away.

**Give me your abbreviated life story.**
Okay, long story short, my story can only be defined as a cautionary tale: never-wait no, ALWAYS bring a towel.

-$0.25

**WORKER ID**
A3U2JWLJ4IAPZ

**What do you do when you are alone?**
I am alone so the first thing on my agenda is to get naked and cook every single item in my refrigerator and closet. Then, I will throw it all over the walls since no one will be around to judge me. Then, I will lick it off the walls and let my dog lick it off the floor.

**Describe your last sexual encounter (use your own definition of "sexual encounter")**
During my last sexual encounter, the guy turned out to have 3 penises instead of one. At first, I thought this would be awkward but it was very convenient and versatile. I used all of them in different positions and it was a lot of fun. After we were done, all 3 of his penises disappeared and it turned into a cucumber.

**What was the last emotion you felt?**
The most recent emotion I felt was sadness because I tried to buy every single pair of shoes in the store today but they were sold out in my size of a few of them so I just left with nothing. If I couldn't buy all 57030350 pairs, then I would be miserable and rather have none. I walked home barefoot while crying.

**A human walking in front of you drops a $20 bill and continues to walk. What do you do?**
I tapped him on the shoulder and told him but he accused me of stealing it from him. Then, he punched me and demanded double the amount of what I found. Instead, I pull my pants down and wiped my ass with it and threw it at him. He ran away quickly.

**Give me your abbreviated life story.**
I have 20 brothers and sisters, all of which are sets of twins. We were all born during a live stage production of our birth while hundreds of people watched and cheered from the audience. Now, we all joined a circus in Las Vegas where we do sibling stunts. I am currently pregnant with quintuplets trying to carry on my family's tradition!

-$0.25

**WORKER ID**
A22I15PKMDDBU5

**What do you do when you are alone?**
I will call all my alien friends from Mars and we will plan for a secret mission of concurring world using all our magic weapons.

**Describe your last sexual encounter (use your own definition of "sexual encounter")**
I was having sexual encounter with two of my friends at the same time. both my friends are biggest enemies of each other. they were in c competition to make me more excited.

**What was the last emotion you felt?**
I was feeling like giving birth to a baby. who will become a superhero and help me to rule the world.

**A human walking in front of you drops a $20 bill and continues to walk. What do you do?**
I will call special intelligence forces to find out out the person and will tell him that his bill was eaten by a cow.

**Give me your abbreviated life story.**
I was born on Pluto. The incident was so pathetic that Pluto vanishes after delivering me to earth. Now i made up my team with aliens from other planets to find out Pluto and rule it again.

-$0.25

**WORKER ID**
A1JV64BL3WCK0G

**What do you do when you are alone?**
I like to spend my alone time organizing things in my house. My pantry is both alphabetized and color-coded.

**Describe your last sexual encounter (use your own definition of "sexual encounter")**
A guy and I hooked up, but it ended poorly. He and I were on were perched on the kitchen table when it gave out under our combined weight, and we tumbled to the floor. I still have the bruise.

**What was the last emotion you felt?**
I felt regret earlier today, finding out that my mom had misunderstood my announcement that I was bringing home dinner. I should have known something was up when she asked me what I wanted. Now, we both have Chinese takeout and too much to eat!

**A human walking in front of you drops a $20 bill and continues to walk. What do you do?**
I would take it and put it toward my engagement ring savings I have been working on. One day, I'll be able to buy a nice ring for myself- not this hunk of junk my fiance got me.

**Give me your abbreviated life story.**
I was born on a small desert island in the Pacific. When I was about 3, my mother and father were able to flag down a passing ship. We moved to Minnesota where I learned how to communicate with elk and wolves. I have now gotten my degree in Communications. I spend my days working as a translator for the National Park Service.

-$0.25

**WORKER ID**
A68CSKRK4XJBX

**What do you do when you are alone?**
I normally sing and dance when I'm by myself. I'm a super musical person but get shy when others are watching.

**Describe your last sexual encounter (use your own definition of "sexual encounter")**
I flirted with a woman in a bar and we made plans for later. She had to use the restroom and then got back--or so I thought. I continued to flirt but it turned out to be a different lady! I was drinking but needless to say, the first woman wasn't pleased when she got back.

**What was the last emotion you felt?**
Anger. I tend to be an irritable person and had an outburst earlier because I broke an omelet while trying to flip it. I'm not great at making eggs.

**A human walking in front of you drops a $20 bill and continues to walk. What do you do?**
I would base my decision on how wealthy they look. I'd only return it if they looked poor. I mean, I'm poor and probably need it more than them.

**Give me your abbreviated life story.**
To make a long story short, I got an engineering degree but somehow wound up working at Starbucks.

-$0.25

## WORKER ID
A1GV0UZU0T2ORS

**What do you do when you are alone?**
I probably masturbate on my belly with my vibrator until I come.

**Describe your last sexual encounter (use your own definition of "sexual encounter")**
I had make up sex with my boyfriend cause we had been arguing. It was a good time as their is always that extra passion in those moments like that.

**What was the last emotion you felt?**
I guess lust or love when I was making love to my boyfriend.

**A human walking in front of you drops a $20 bill and continues to walk. What do you do?**
I would probably tell the person unless they were really far away. I might just keep it. Might depend on the mood I am in and how much the person seems to need it.

**Give me your abbreviated life story.**
I have a Bachelor's degree. I grew up in the midwestern suburbs. I have played poker part time for a living which is odd for a girl. I love to draw, paint, play guitar and piano, and pretty much get involved with a lot of creative stuff. I am a freak in bed and love sex.

-$0.25

12

**WORKER ID**
A2Z6Y7MS2ZNTC5

**What do you do when you are alone?**
When I am alone I love to talk to my other-dimensional selves and give myself advice or just hear myself talk about whats going on in the other universes.

**Describe your last sexual encounter (use your own definition of "sexual encounter")**
During my last sexual encounter my headboard broke away from the wall and fell on my face just as I was reaching climax. It was not the worst orgasm I've had but far from the best for sure.

**What was the last emotion you felt?**
The most recent emotional I felt was pure joy as I watched a youtube video of a mother singing to her infant son and the baby appears to go through all kinds of emotions.

**A human walking in front of you drops a $20 bill and continues to walk. What do you do?**
I would avoid touching it because I am allergic to paper money. I only use coins when I need to spend cash.

**Give me your abbreviated life story.**
I was born in West Philadelphia and raised by a single mother. Pretty normal childhood but got bullied a bit. After one really bad fight at school while playing basketball for PE my mom decided it was too much to handle so she sent me to live with my uncle and aunt in California. I took a taxi to their huge house and was greeted by a butler. I spent the next few years getting into lots of trouble with my cousins and here I am now.

-$0.25

**WORKER ID**
A2I6OHA5UXITYS

## What's your most visited website?

My most visited website is https://us.teletubbies.com/. I literally visit it at least a hundred times per day because I am 110% certain that there is some sort of code in each of their shapes on their big heads. One of these days, I swear I will figure out what the hell the shapes REALLY mean and who or what is trying to communicate with me as I visit the website and see their flashing faces. Pure evil I tell you!

## What happened to your face?

In 1997 I was 16 years old. At school during drama practice, a friend (let's call her Tamber) and I were making faces at one another during our down time when neither of us had lines in our play. We had a bet going on--Tamber bet me that she could create an uglier face than I could, but I thought she was wrong. If I won, she had to humiliate herself in front of the group by dancing wildly and making animal noises while the others were practicing their lines. If she won, I had to write a paper for her biology class. Well, we both made our faces and asked classmates to judge. The problem is that we held our faces in that position for at least 10-20 minutes because people were coming and going. Mom was right, my face will stay like that if I leave it for too long. It was all for nothing anyway, Tamber won and I wrote her paper about genetic mutations.

## Name of your first pet?

I had a bird that I named Marco. I used to let Marco fly all over the house without a cage. When I wanted to find him, I would yell "Marco!" and he would reply "Pollo"! It was fun until one day he failed to reply. RIP Marco.

## What was your high school prom like?

My high school prom was amazing--it was an under the sea theme in a large boat with an upperdeck for dancing and an underwater cabin that was enormous where it was catered with another small dance floor that was more intimate. I did not have a date, so I didn't exactly attend. I rented some scuba gear and decided to prank everyone by wearing a super-realistic shark costume. I mean, it was amazing with sharp teeth and smooth skin. I paid the band to play the Jaws theme at a certain time of the night. Someone had smuggled in alcohol, so it was even more hilarious because the drunk classmates were easily fooled. I paid someone to also

14

scream that the boat was sinking and make a huge BOOM! right before. At least 10 people jumped overboard. Luckily, someone saved the drunk ones before anything happened. No one ever found out it was me!

**Who is your greatest enemy?**
My evil nemesis is named Alexia. Her mission in life seems to be to make mine HELL. She ran over me with her car once and blamed ME for it. At one point she overheard me talking about a job I wanted to apply to and she applied and got the job. While in a class, if I get a 100 on a test she says she got 101. I bought a new, 2016 car recently. She drove up right after and mentioned she bought a new car as well and it was a 2017. Last week I lost 3 lbs, but she came into work and said she lost 5 lbs. She always tries to one-up me and it's annoying. She screwed up paperwork one day and was able to somehow convince the boss that it was all because I had incorrectly instructed her on what to do. I hadn't even talked to her that day!!! She is my greatest enemy!

-$0.25

**WORKER ID**
A5DSYVNGYLCA5

**What's your most visited website?**
most visited website is an facebook to chat with friends and so many things
to fast updates

**What happened to your face?**
it's an link of oppurtunity to chat with doesn't know her persons on that
face

**Name of your first pet?**
potato

**What was your high school prom like?**
high school prom is really fantastic with dance and cultures

**Who is your greatest enemy?**
no one is enemy all are my friends

-$0.25

**WORKER ID**
A1XACRIZ51TBMY

**What's your most visited website?**
Balletshoes.com  because sometimes a brother just wants to dance.

**What happened to your face?**
This was the long term result of global warming.

**Name of your first pet?**
Pookie

**What was your high school prom like?**
Which one? I faked being a teenager while in my 20's. I graduated again under an alias all because I liked going to proms so much

**Who is your greatest enemy?**
Dr. Octopuss

-$0.25

**WORKER ID**
A23CTGXNDDW5LC

**What's your most visited website?**
My most visited website is the Hamster Dance website (url: http://www.hamsterdance.org/hamsterdance/ ). I visit it frequently because I find the image of the many hamsters dancing in unison to the jaunty, melodic tune to be very soothing for me mentally and emotionally. I spend hours staring at the screen, transfixed.

**What happened to your face?**
Unfortunately, many years ago, it was decided that my unparalleled beauty posed a public health risk for those around me, as people who passed by me would get caught up staring at me in admiration and not look where they were going or totally forget what they were doing. This led to many car accidents, injuries from accidental falls, and other damages. As a result, the local legislature passed a bill mandating that I undergo surgery to reconstruct my face to look like a regular person's. I probably could have taken this issue to the Supreme Court as a violation of my individual rights, but luckily I am also very humble and selfless so I decided to accept the decision and undergo the surgery for the good of my community. That's why my face looks so regular now.

**Name of your first pet?**
My childhood pet was named "Pet Nixon." Naturally, I chose this name as a punny tribute to America's beloved former first lady, wife to our greatest president Mr. Richard Nixon. Pet Nixon was an african pygmy hedgehog. I adopted her at age three and chose that name to honor my role model, Lady Nixon.

**What was your high school prom like?**
My high school prom was a disaster. Somehow, our school ended up hiring the wrong DJ and this guy just played Barry Manilow songs all night long. We all just sat there awkwardly sipping the lukewarm punch they served us. Nobody danced except for a few kids who were trying to be polite and not make the guy feel bad about his DJ performance. He really loved Barry Manilow and was really getting into his set, so it was nice that those kids honored his passion like that.

**Who is your greatest enemy?**
My greatest enemy is my upstairs neighbor in my apartment building. All night long he paces back and forth and seems to always be rearranging his furniture at obscure hours. He also has a pet duck, who he allows to roam freely throughout the building. One time I saw the duck out on my fire escape peering into my window. I swear that thing is a spy. I'll need to procure a duck of my own. I refuse to be defeated.

-$0.25

**WORKER ID**
AJTAAGXRG14UA

**What's your most visited website?**
Bestgore is the most visited website. I love to see someone's face get impaled.

**What happened to your face?**
The gods of beauty determined that I would be the best candidate for the world's best looking face.

**Name of your first pet?**
Sam. We named him in honor of my uncle who died in Stalingrad.

**What was your high school prom like?**
I only danced with girls who had a date.

**Who is your greatest enemy?**
Bigot Republicans who think capitalism is the best economic system.

-$0.25

**WORKER ID**
A2T50IRD435JRZ

**What's your most visited website?**
Its pornhub. They have videos lots of highly creative people doing interesting stuffs to themselves!

**What happened to your face?**
I was supposed to be rescued by Batman from a bomb explosion, but that shit hole went and rescued his damn good for nothing girlfriend.

**Name of your first pet?**
Mister Gross. My pet dog was so ugly that I had to call him that.

**What was your high school prom like?**
I had no memory. The whole event was drenched with drug that no one remembered!

**Who is your greatest enemy?**
Frodo. That idiot destroyed the ring I wanted.

- $0.25

**WORKER ID**
A1NOGVJ7O47lOO

**What's your most visited website?**
I like to frequent the Dip n Dots website. I send as many emails as possible every day because I have so many questions about what I'm supposed to do with my life. They are the ice cream of the future and I just think the technology is so advanced that we can email people in the future that send us ice cream from the future.

**What happened to your face?**
When I was a kid, I grew up in India and I was snake charmer at 10. My snake, Nigel, turned on me one day because they didn't have the kind of mouse he liked at the store.

**Name of your first pet?**
We named my pet monkey, Sir Charles Worthington III.

**What was your high school prom like?**
I hate talking about this because it's really embarrassing. I was wearing this super hot dress and having a great time, until, I started feeling really weird. It turns out someone put acid in the punch bowl. I ended up licking the principals face calling him my Mint Chocolate Surprise.

**Who is your greatest enemy?**
He is a small frog that turns into a dragon that lives in my attic. His name is Preston and he comes in my room and calls me names and we battle every night. I never get any sleep.

-$0.25

**WORKER ID**
A3V2XOIEVMYEBQ

**What's your most visited website?**
I often go on Tinder because I'm always on the look out for someone to go out with. Its hard to find sexy older gentlemen into classy, older women -- especially older gentlemen that are curious about other ways to use catheters. I find Tinder the best place to go looking.

**What happened to your face?**
When I was little, I had a pet guinea pig, Rosey. I would make sure to place her back in her cage every night so that she wouldn't get lost. One night, I woke up in the middle of the night and felt something furry on my face. I thought it was the cat. I opened my eyes and as they focused, I saw Rosey perched on my nose. I began to smile and then Rosey attacked. She bit down, hard, on my nose and it was a long hard battle to get her off. I kept the scars to remind me to never trust small mammals.

**Name of your first pet?**
My mom got a pet cat, Venus, from a coworker. She was an adult cat and she was huge and very angry. She hated everyone. No one wanted to pet her or anything because she'd either run away or swat. Well, I made it my personal mission to befriend that angry Venus. I got scratched, hissed at, bitten... but I kept trying to simply pet her. I would start by sitting next to her and then she eventually let me pet her. And finally, after many months, she purred when I touched her and thereafter she lived up to her name Venus, goddess of love (at least towards me).

**What was your high school prom like?**
I made it a point to wear a tux when I went 'stag'. It was kind of expensive and no one other than my friends understood why I, an otherwise femme girl, wanted to wear a tux. Well, I just did. There's something appealing about a girl in a tux, you know? Long story short, people gave me some long looks at the start but by the end, no one was interested anymore and I spilled a lot of punch on that tux.

**Who is your greatest enemy?**
There's this girl that shares my somewhat uncommon name, Jacquelyn. We've gone to school together since elementary school and we've been enemies for almost as long. It all started one day in middle school. I was

rushing to class, it was past the bell, and I was going to be late. I slammed my locker shut and started to run to class. Then I tripped and fell, my books and things spilling all over the floor. I gasped and looked around for the source of my clumsiness. "Oh my gosh, are you okay?" I hear behind me and whip my head around with a glare that could wither roses. She offered me a hand up and I grabbed my stuff and accepted. And then I realized I had tripped over her as she had been kneeling on the ground. She smiled as she helped me to my feet and brushed me off. I hated her ever since.

-$0.25

**WORKER ID**
A2SFAW068VC8C6

**How do you make money?**
To make money, I perform at our local skating rink - dancing the Waltz to the song "Tennessee Waltz" and getting the train line going to "The Locomotion."  Its mainly for tips but I can pick up extra cash by manning the pizza oven.

**What's that smell?**
That would be my patchouli and garlic air freshener.  There is nothing better than the smell of burning oak leaves and sauteed garlic to relax you after a long day at work.

**When was the last time you washed your human hands?**
My human hands were washed a couple of days ago after I touched that shopping cart in Walmart.  My monkey hands were washed just this morning after I ate a pork cake for breakfast.

**Who would win in a fight: you, or a more confident and attractive version of you?**
Although my more confident version of myself thinks she can beat me in a fight, she's too pretty for her own good and I will knock her cutsie self into next week by putting her in a figure four leg lock and tickling her feet.

**Human Granny just asked if you can keep a secret. Can you?**
Grandma, I can keep a secret!  I live in your basement and see virtually no one and your secrets are a bit boring anyway.

-$0.25

**WORKER ID**
TURKOPTICON

**REQUESTER**
A1AJ35NTQ1DARP

**FAIR**
1/5

**FAST**
1/5

**PAY**
1/5

**COMM**
1/5

**REVIEW**
Requester had a hit about creativity.
Rejected saying I wasn't creative enough.
Creativity is subjective. Considering this, he can reject all workers answers.
After making me work on his hit, he rejected 0.25 $, with this fake reason?

To be avoided!

**REFLECTION**
I suppose my criteria for creativity were too stringent.

All the same, I can't help but feel like this dude's a dick

+/- $0.00

## WORKER ID
A2OZO0I3XX690K

**How do you make money?**
My husband doesn't know that I put a portion of my paycheck in a secret personal account. In fact, I put more of that there than in our joint account. When I want something, I take money from there. I'm loaded.

**What's that smell?**
I've been experimenting in the kitchen. It's coffee marinated salmon. Mmmm.

**When was the last time you washed your human hands?**
It's been at least 24 hours. I applied this expensive prescription ointment to it for my arthritis, and I'm afraid of washing it off. It'd be like washing money down the drain.

**Who would win in a fight: you, or a more confident and attractive version of you?**
The confident, attractive version. of me. I'd be so under the spell of his aura that I'd go weak, and attractive me would knock me out.

**Human Granny just asked if you can keep a secret. Can you?**
Yes, of course. Hacking is my hobby, and I keep all of those secrets I find there. I even have Donald Trump's tax returns that I'm waiting to give to Wikileaks.

-$0.25

**WORKER ID**
AEY67OL8UKB

**How do you make money?**
I normally get money from trees.

**What's that smell?**
That nasty smell is from a perfume.

**When was the last time you washed your human hands?**
I washed my hands last year.

**Who would win in a fight: you, or a more confident and attractive version of you?**
I will win a fight. I win the fight by talking.

**Human Granny just asked if you can keep a secret. Can you?**
I can keep a secret by telling others immediately.

-$0.25

**WORKER ID**
A3PD06OTVDYTQN

**How do you make money?**
I spend each day during the school year teaching children to be disrespectful, disobedient slackers. I am a great teacher.

**What's that smell?**
It is the presence of Farticus, the Greek god of flatulence. You must have made an offering to him.

**When was the last time you washed your human hands?**
Do you mean before or after I became infected? Thinking back, it was probably some time before I took a crap but after I made your salad.

**Who would win in a fight: you, or a more confident and attractive version of you?**
I would win. I would literally beat the hell out of the attractive version of myself because I am made she is just now showing up.

**Human Granny just asked if you can keep a secret. Can you?**
Sure thing, Grandma. Consider me your verbal Depend. No leaks.

-$0.25

**WORKER ID**
A2BLA8KJIAMXTW

**How do you make money?**
I sell breast milk by the ounce to fetishists and to people who want to feed their children breast milk but cannot produce their own.

**What's that smell?**
Its curry, sorry.  My roommate is obsessed with curry.

**When was the last time you washed your human hands?**
The last time I washed my human hands was before the accident, 6 years ago.  I now have prosthetic limbs, but do wash them regularly.

**Who would win in a fight: you, or a more confident and attractive version of you?**
I would win, because I wouldn't be worried about keeping up my appearances.  I would dropkick my snooty self.

**Human Granny just asked if you can keep a secret. Can you?**
No.  I'm a big blabbermouth.

-$0.25

**WORKER ID**
A17J1CE7N49Z9D

**How do you make money?**
i get money by selling eliphants door to door

**What's that smell?**
that smell are birds eating a fart

**When was the last time you washed your human hands?**
i has never washed my hands

**Who would win in a fight: you, or a more confident and attractive version of you?**
i would win due to the powers i have

**Human Granny just asked if you can keep a secret. Can you?**
i can keep a secret as well as a magician can to a spork

-$0.25

**REJECTED WORKER ID**
A1AJ35NTQ1DARP

**THOUGHTS**
Well, Amazon Mechanical Turk has made the decision to keep me away from working for them. Their criteria for choosing their workers is proprietary, so I will instead take some time to guess why I wasn't chosen.

I'm a dime a dozen.

I am proud of being very good at video games and ashamed of my inability to shower regularly.

I'm insecure about where I can apply for a job, and the prospect of working virtually speaks to a reality I've always dreamed of.

I want to be plugged in.

I want to be paid for it.

+/- $0.00

**WORKER ID**
A3FPXLLF0B8CIC

**How do you make money?**
I fly a drone into banks and scoop it up

**What's that smell?**
It's most likely alien poop

**When was the last time you washed your human hands?**
When I actually had some

**Who would win in a fight: you, or a more confident and attractive version of you?**
Win? I think they would tie.

**Human Granny just asked if you can keep a secret. Can you?**
The alien grandma just spilled the secret.

-$0.25

**WORKER ID**
A23CTGXNDDW5LC

### How do you make money?
I normally get money by robbing my local bank. At this point, they recognize my face so they know the drill right when I walk in and just start putting the money into a bag for me. It's really convenient. I'm surprised more people don't think of this.

### What's that smell?
It is obviously the smell of the chemicals the federal government is spraying all over this country. You can see the trails in the sky as proof.

### When was the last time you washed your human hands?
It has been 7 years since I last washed my human hands. I got to meet the president 7 years ago, and he shook both of my hands, one hand for hello and the other for goodbye. I wanted to preserve the memory forever, so I vowed to never wash these human hands of mine ever again. I wear three pairs of waterproof gloves at all times to ensure this.

### Who would win in a fight: you, or a more confident and attractive version of you?
I would win the fight against the more attractive, confident version of myself. I would win by placing a large mirror in front of her and telling her that she was so pretty and wonderful and infallible that I could obviously never fight her. Being confident and attractive, she would feel that this explanation made sense and then start admiring herself in the mirror. That is when I would attack and achieve victory through the element of surprise.

### Human Granny just asked if you can keep a secret. Can you?
Technically, yes, I can keep a secret. However, I will not keep a secret for human grandma. I refuse. I will tell everyone anything she tells me.

-$0.25

**WORKER ID**
A8VAJKHA3AA7J

**How do you make money?**
I purchased a fake police badge and I tell all the pan handlers to give me all of their money or I will arrest them.

**What's that smell?**
It is probably the diaper that my baby shoved in the back of the fridge.

**When was the last time you washed your human hands?**
Who washes their hands?

**Who would win in a fight: you, or a more confident and attractive version of you?**
I would win because I would be pissed off that he looked better than me, so I'd knock his ass out.  He won't look better than me with a missing tooth.

**Human Granny just asked if you can keep a secret. Can you?**
I'll keep her secrets as long as I'm happy with how much money she is going to leave me when she dies.  If she ain't paying up, I'll sell her secrets to the highest bidder.

-$0.25

**WORKER ID**
AQK9RIOA9FURX

**Which mummy is the best mummy?**
Ramsey is the best mummy because he was wrapped up the tightest using the most advanced form of embalmbing.

**Where are you right now?**
I am currently in the Florida Keys. I took a plan down here to go diving to escape the cold snap in the Northeast.

**How tightly do you hug?**
I don't touch other humans unless I am in a full HazMat suit.

**Why are the yams so dry?**
The yams are so dry because I ran out of regular milk so I used breastmilk.

**What will you be remembered for?**
I will be remembered for the 4th of July bash last year. My town never saw as many trucks, cops, firefighters and fireworks in one place.

-$0.25

**WORKER ID**
A3UITZ4R9EE75I

**Which mummy is the best mummy?**
King Tut is best because they came back to life to guard his tomb from tomb robber.

**Where are you right now?**
I am at my house which is on top of the Himalayas mountains.

**How tightly do you hug?**
As tight as possible until we merge into one person.

**Why are the yams so dry?**
Yams are so dry because little flies live inside that sucked in all the water inside.

**What will you be remembered for?**
I will be remember for being the smartest human in the world and finding the cure for cancer. And finding life in other planets.

-$0.25

**REJECTED WORKER ID**
A1AJ35NTQ1DARP

**THOUGHTS**
I will break even. I've decided to apply for ur-jobs, but once again I refuse to leave this room.

Rev.com is a transcription service that lets me get paid $0.65 per minute of audio that I transcribe. Hoo wee. Seems fine.

They gave me a handy Google Doc to help me with the application.

I can see the people who are also looking at the Doc:


**49 total viewers**

**Anonymous Capybara**
**Anonymous Cormorant**
**Anonymous Elepghant**
**Anonymous Ibex**
**Anonymous Iguana**
**Anonymous Kangaroo**


I'm not alone!

Yes!

Wait!

Shit!

**+/- $0.00**

## WORKER ID
A11DOB7V9YBL4S

## Which mummy is the best mummy?
My mates mum because she gives him chocolate to take to work everyday, lucky guy!

## Where are you right now?
I am sitting in a deck chair on the moon admiring the earth.

## How tightly do you hug?
I hug them until their dinner from the previous night comes back up.

## Why are the yams so dry?
Because they are given special air dry treatment in the middle of the night when nobody is looking.

## What will you be remembered for?
As the man that can eat a lemon whilst roller blading on the surface of the ocean.

-$0.25

**WORKER ID**
A6QMYJ1FWU9QA

**Which mummy is the best mummy?**
King Tut is the one of the best mummies, because his wrap is made of cursed material and he comes to life at a certain year.

**Where are you right now?**
I am hanging onto the side of my roof, using my laptop, cause my signal is bad and I have to make some Amazon Turk money.

**How tightly do you hug?**
I hug my humans until they pass out from being hugged so tightly, because I have started working out.

**Why are the yams so dry?**
Yams are a dry potato because it suck alot of water out of the ground and it is always dehydrated.

**What will you be remembered for?**
i have a large stone, that I have been ingraving slowly for my tomb.

-$0.25

**WORKER ID**
AUR6U2RJAGUTF

## Which mummy is the best mummy?
Egyptian mummy is the best mummy because it is stuffed for hundreds of years.

## Where are you right now?
Well my mind is wondering over the mountains of Himalaya but my body is still in my bed

## How tightly do you hug?
Tight enough that they choke on my love

## Why are the yams so dry?
The yams are dry because they are gifts from the Egyptian mummies.

## What will you be remembered for?
I will be remembered as someone who will never be forgotten

-$0.25

**WORKER ID**
A17J1CE7N49Z9D

**Which mummy is the best mummy?**
the best mummy is the one that feeds you

**Where are you right now?**
im in Narnia

**How tightly do you hug?**
i hug like a drink would hug a cow

**Why are the yams so dry?**
yams are as dry as my moist water

**What will you be remembered for?**
like a dragon in the sea

-$0.25

**WORKER ID**
A1SMAPOIC2E7YH

### Which mummy is the best mummy?
Mummy who doesn't let his son  live is the best kind of mummy because she protects him from going to school and doing lots of homework.

### Where are you right now?
I'm on mercury planet right now making a barbeque and hanging out with my friend but I'll be back in a few days.

### How tightly do you hug?
Mostly i hug people not because of some warm feelings for them but to dislocate their shoulder.

### Why are the yams so dry?
Yams are dry because if a yam reacts with water it becomes a highly toxic chemical that can kill us in seconds.

### What will you be remembered for?
I will be remembered because i killed the real anaconda with just my right hand and protected the whole world from annihilation.

-$0.25

**WORKER ID**
A1AJ35NTQ1DARP

**THOUGHTS**
I got an email from WORKER ID: A1SMAPOIC2E7YH:

Respected sir
I really like doing your HITs   .Can   I please attempt some more?
Yours sincerely

Made my heart flutter

+/- $0.00

**WORKER ID**
A1OK974KXKO6FJ

**Which mummy is the best mummy?**
The one which lives under my house. He comes out sometimes and chases me around the yard. We have lots of fun together.

**Where are you right now?**
I am standing on top of the Eiffel Tower.

**How tightly do you hug?**
only until their eyes start to bulge. Any harder and they pop.

**Why are the yams so dry?**
They are grown in the Sahara desert and there is no water there.

**What will you be remembered for?**
As the first person to set foot on Mars in their pajamas.

-$0.25

**WORKER ID**
A29HS8UKNCMCQU

**What are you wearing right now?**
I AM WEARING A ONE PIECE RED UNION SUIT, WITH THE FLAP OPEN
IN THE BACK AND 16INCH RUBBER BOOTS, WHILE PAINTING MY
FRONT PORCH.

**What is your most attractive feature?**
I REALLY CAN'T DECIDE BETWEEN MY 4 INCH NOSE OR BY FLOPPY
EARS.

**What do you say when you want to impress people?**
WATCH THIS, IT DIDNT HURT.

**Where's the money?**
IN THE MEAT LOCKER, NEXT TO THE BEEF.

**What's the worst thing you have walked in on?**
A DEAF WOMEN GIVEN A BLIND MAN A BJ. SHE COULD NOT HEAR
ME AND HE COULD NOT SEE ME.

-$0.25

**WORKER ID**
A3EJI3R6ZE9Y4X

**What are you wearing right now?**
All I am wearing is a strategically located sock.

**What is your most attractive feature?**
I would have to say that my most attractive feature is my complete lack of a face.

**What do you say when you want to impress people?**
You've never met anyone with as many extra nipples as me.

**Where's the money?**
I ate it. All of it.

**What's the worst thing you have walked in on?**
One time when I was a child, I woke up in the middle of the night, and I heard my father grunting in the living room. Curious me got up and walked in there to see what was going on, and there he was. Sweaty. No shirt. He was sawing logs by hand right there in our living room.

-$0.25

**WORKER ID**
ALDQRWYZ8KQ9A

**What are you wearing right now?**
I adamantly refuse to wear pants when I'm at home. And I'm currently at home. I also won't wear shirts. Or much of anything, actually. So I'm currently only wearing a pair of glasses and a sock on my package (don't ask me why). I'm also wearing a lot of eye shadow. Does that count?

**What is your most attractive feature?**
My most attractive feature is my personality, otherwise known as my cherry red Porsche 911. My personality cost $200,000.

**What do you say when you want to impress people?**
If I want to impress someone I tell them that I invented the Filet-o-Fish.

**Where's the money?**
I keep the money in my sock drawer, in the form of silver bars, rare stamps, and nude photos of Oprah.

**What's the worst thing you have walked in on?**
I could not believe this. One day I went into the bathroom at work and there was my boss, standing in front of the urinal, with his pants around his ankles. I swear to goodness. He was a grown man and he'd taken his pants and underwear and dropped them all the way down to the floor while he took a piss, like he was some 5-year-old who didn't have the coordination to do otherwise. Somehow he still managed to pee on his own shoes.

-$0.25

**WORKER ID**
AZZZYAYJQSDOJ

**What are you wearing right now?**
A blow up samurai costume from Halloween. My husband loves it when I dress up in it and he gets to deflate me.

**What is your most attractive feature?**
I let my leg hair grow so long that people that have a thing for a squatch really love them.

**What do you say when you want to impress people?**
I went to modeling school and use to model in Paris.

**Where's the money?**
The guy with the ice cream truck has it stuffed in his freezer, right below the push ups.

**What's the worst thing you have walked in on?**
There they were stabbing the Donald Trump doll over and over while screaming...dump the Trump, dump the Trump.

-$0.25

**WORKER ID**
A2M3LVBUZLN8MO

**What are you wearing right now?**
I am not wearing anything right now because my dog ate my clothes.

**What is your most attractive feature?**
I would have to say my muscles because they are so big they are
hard to miss.

**What do you say when you want to impress people?**
I tell people I am rich because I own an old car and avoid car
payments.

**Where's the money?**
The money is all around me just sitting there.

**What's the worst thing you have walked in on?**
I walked in on my uncle watching days of our lives.

-$0.25

**WORKER ID**
A2LZ9KG42SZ3I0

**What are you wearing right now?**
I am wearing a pink dress I won from Hulk Hogan.

**What is your most attractive feature?**
I have beautiful green eyes, they were black until I dyed them.

**What do you say when you want to impress people?**
I say I am a poor immigrant to get money.

**Where's the money?**
It is hiddden in the monastery.

**What's the worst thing you have walked in on?**
I once walked in on pinnochio and a tree having relations.

-$0.25

**WORKER ID**
A1V1BWPEQX90X1

**What are you wearing right now?**
Mostly dog hair - my Chow/Husky cross is shedding big time!

**What is your most attractive feature?**
my mouth - it constantly attracts chocolate

**What do you say when you want to impress people?**
I tell them I can run run a mile in under 8.  I dont mention that I mean 8 hours

**Where's the money?**
If I knew the answer to that I wouldn't be working on a 25c hit!

**What's the worst thing you have walked in on?**
a  big spider in the pantry

-$0.25

**WORKER ID**
AKHO08K69B4Y4

**You've been given an extra arm. What do you do with it?**
I would keep that as a spare in my drawer and replace my right arm
in two years from now. My right arm has a disease that gradually
turns it purple. When all of it is completely purple the arm will start
to emit smoke and then turn black and die. So at that time, the extra
hand will be different, I don't want to be a weird guy with only one
hand!

**What would your hands say if they could talk?**
Oh! They would definitely try to turn me in for the murders I had
them do for me. Juts for revenge...

**What is the largest human gathering you have been a part of?**
I have been part of the 1st gathering of gardeners on moon. The
gathering was legendary big because all sort of creatures from
around the galaxy came. In fact, it was the first intergalactic meeting
on nay matter!

**What is your favorite movie?**
My favorite movie is on the "murdering my boss". It's the third movie
from the sequel of Alice in wonderland and the main character is the
Rabbit, talking about his life, his work and his struggle to keep work
life and sex life in distance.

**Which animal is the best animal?**
The best animal is azu ghosts. Azu ghost is not offcourse a ghost
(since ghosts does not actually exist) but he is a holographic pet you
can rent or get from the donations section for free. The actual pet
lives on the Azu planet, which is a planet full of Azus, just playing all
day. You rent it and have it whenever it suits you as a hologram.

-$0.25

**WORKER ID**
A2X6K5T4P6GXTY

**You've been given an extra arm. What do you do with it?**
I will pretend as a God-Man and would start a business pretending to be the messenger of God.

**What would your hands say if they could talk?**
It will say the good and bad works that we had done with it in the past.

**What is the largest human gathering you have been a part of?**
I went to attend the Tomorrowland DJ party, which was the largest gathering I had ever been to.

**What is your favorite movie?**
My favorite movie is the Prestige, also I like all the Christopher Nolan movies.

**Which animal is the best animal?**
I think Lion is the best animal based on the beauty this animal possess.

-$0.25

**WORKER ID**
A3MS21UJPMHLK0

**You've been given an extra arm. What do you do with it?**
I would use it to beat the person I hate to death.

**What would your hands say if they could talk?**
"You know, you really shouldn't use that kind of lotion on your skin. It smells gross!"

**What is the largest human gathering you have been a part of?**
I was a part of a cult, once. I left as soon as a meeting was called and we were to drink koolaid.

**What is your favorite movie?**
I really, really liked Frozen. I find the songs very catchy and I never grow tired of them.

**Which animal is the best animal?**
I think the dog is the best animal. I absolutely despise cats.

-$0.25

**WORKER ID**
A17J1CE7N49Z9D

**You've been given an extra arm. What do you do with it?**
i eat it

**What would your hands say if they could talk?**
they would say they want to be a dinosaur

**What is the largest human gathering you have been a part of?**
i was part of a million dollar army

**What is your favorite movie?**
the movie with a vampire that eats cabbage and garlic

**Which animal is the best animal?**
the best animal is the gradonzee

-$0.25

**WORKER ID**
A1SMAPOIC2E7YH

**You've been given an extra arm. What do you do with it?**
I will play a multiplayer game with myself on PlayStation.

**What would your hands say if they could talk?**
They would ask me to stop using them all the time and give them some space.

**What is the largest human gathering you have been a part of?**
The largest crowd I've faced was when I became the president of USA this year.

**What is your favorite movie?**
My favourite movie is "The Mask" because it was my first appearance in Hollywood as an actor.

**Which animal is the best animal?**
My favourite animal is a Pig because it can be used as a piggy bank and we can make some good dishes from it.

-$0.25

**WORKER ID**
A5DSYVNGYLCA5

**You've been given an extra arm. What do you do with it?**
to show all humans with very protest

**What would your hands say if they could talk?**
hands for using mainly eating and slapping some one

**What is the largest human gathering you have been a part of?**
i have ever been a part of largest human gathering is eating.

**What is your favorite movie?**
i like cartoon movie

**Which animal is the best animal?**
i like axe in forest

-$0.25

**WORKER ID**
A3HJC6BU35CPE0

**You've been given an extra arm. What do you do with it?**
I do not have a handful of mechanical skills like drawing and
carpentry, so I could use an extra arm to help me learn those.

**What would your hands say if they could talk?**
I want to slap somebody!

**What is the largest human gathering you have been a part of?**
The cemetery is a large gathering of interesting persons if you want
to meet somebody and age will probably matter.

**What is your favorite movie?**
Watching the paint dry is so interesting!

**Which animal is the best animal?**
It would have to be the sphynx.

-$0.25

**WORKER ID**
A3JTMXHPNCUFNX

**You've been given an extra arm. What do you do with it?**
I keep it shoved inside my shirt becaus it is embarrasing and you have no idea how hard it is making shirts for my third arm.

**What would your hands say if they could talk?**
Yuck, I smell like Cheetos and am all orange.

**What is the largest human gathering you have been a part of?**
Oh, I went to one of those Christian revivals in Alabama a few years ago. There was like 50,000 people there speaking in tongues.

**What is your favorite movie?**
I have never seen a movie in my whole life. My family doesn't believe in tv or entertainment.

**Which animal is the best animal?**
Obviously the rat is the best animal since they are so cute and cuddly. They are mostly disease free and have the cutest tails.

-$0.25

**REJECTED WORKER ID**
A1AJ35NTQ1DARP

**THOUGHTS**
It didn't take long to get the right workflow going for the transcription.

I've listened to this conversation about screwdrivers and paint roller poles more time than any human was ever intended to.

There are at least 48 other humans listening to this boring conversation.

Comforting.

+/- $0.00

**WORKER ID**
A2RVUSQQ0150J2

**What purpose does art serve in society?**
It's a great source of fiber.

**Do you have any experience with potted plants?**
I'm wearing one on my head now

**How do you feel about your human body?**
I feel pretty good about it as a meal or light snack.

**What was your favorite subject in human school?**
I really enjoyed studying for my detention class.

**Where did you grow up?**
Beneath the ocean, until I turned 5. Then, I went to elementary school on the moon.

-$0.25

**WORKER ID**
A1N4P4XGQM7NXE

**What purpose does art serve in society?**
Art serves no purpose in a society that can produce a president trump. Creativity is a lie.

**Do you have any experience with potted plants?**
Yes. I have an extensive background in all things potted and plantlike, due to my time in the war.

**How do you feel about your human body?**
I feel that its the pinnacle of creation, and a testament to gods gifts that I am blessed to move around in each day.

**What was your favorite subject in human school?**
MY favorite subject was math, because I was so good at it! I went on to use it in most every aspect of my life, and frequently apply it whenever I can.

**Where did you grow up?**
The streets of bololvia. It was a hard knock life, but I turned out ok.

-$0.25

**WORKER ID**
A2UNSF09FWX9S8

**What purpose does art serve in society?**
Art is a way to create employment for people who just can't cut it in society. It gives these people a dignified way to occupy their time.

**Do you have any experience with potted plants?**
I worked for 18 months for a potter making specialty plastic pots. As part of our testing program I was required to plant seedlings in the pots and monitor their growth.

**How do you feel about your human body?**
After a decade of constant effort I now have the ability to completely control my body at the cellular level. I can go days without taknig a breath.

**What was your favorite subject in human school?**
In 9th grade I had an exchange teacher for PE. He taught us the art of Judo.

**Where did you grow up?**
From age 1 till age 17 I lived on the top floor of a turn-of-the-century highrise building in downtown Minneapolis. The building had a store and an indoor playground. I didn't leave the building until the age of 7.

-$0.25

**WORKER ID**
A2089GGBHBLVSQ

**What purpose does art serve in society?**
It helps to know what kind of thing to buy when you are a very rich man and you don't want to look like vulgar.

**Do you have any experience with potted plants?**
No, I have always been afraid the plant grow so big and then the pott explode.

**How do you feel about your human body?**
I think I am a alien.

**What was your favorite subject in human school?**
Biology, so I coul get animals organ apart.

**Where did you grow up?**
The only thing i know is that I didn't grow up inside a pott

-$0.25

**WORKER ID**
A1SMAPOIC2E7YH

**What purpose does art serve in society?**
Art has an important functions in society as it helps in curing lung cancer.

**Do you have any experience with potted plants?**
I planted a flower plant in a pot but it turned out to be carnivorous in nature and aate my pet.

**How do you feel about your human body?**
A body is a complex structure capable of doiing a number of things like flying.

**What was your favorite subject in human school?**
Compuer science was my suject in the school because teachers knew that i won't learn it by myself and had to be taught.

**Where did you grow up?**
I grew up on Kryptonite and superman was my cousin brother.

-$0.25

**WORKER ID**
AQE6A9JJM7FZM

**What purpose does art serve in society?**
Art serves a great deals in society. Not only it helps solve crimes, but also, it defines the guidelines that police investigators and detectives use to analyze evidence.

**Do you have any experience with potted plants?**
I have once eaten a potted plant, which cause me diarrhea and ended up in the hospital.

**How do you feel about your human body?**
I feel that my human body is the most twisted creation of all times. It is misshaped and ambiguous.

**What was your favorite subject in human school?**
I love mathematics. They show me deep meanings to my everyday life.

**Where did you grow up?**
I grew up in Rwanda.

-$0.25

**WORKER ID**
A3ES4BXB8PJWTX

**What purpose does art serve in society?**
It serves no function other than feeding the artist's ego.

**Do you have any experience with potted plants?**
I don't really know what that is.

**How do you feel about your human body?**
I think physical strength is something that separates people who deserve to live from those who don't. I try to become as strong as I can be.


**What was your favorite subject in human school?**
Physics because it achieves what philosophy aspires to become.

**Where did you grow up?**
I grew up in the city of zarqa in Jordan.

-$0.25

**WORKER ID**
AD1ILDUXZHASF

**What purpose does art serve in society?**
Art just gives people something to look at when they feel bored.

**Do you have any experience with potted plants?**
Yes, I had a cactus for a while, until I overwatered it.

**How do you feel about your human body?**
I hate my body. I keep on getting sick all the time, I'm weak and I smell kind of funky.

**What was your favorite subject in human school?**
My favorite subject was math. I love to just find cheats in math, it's so easy. It all makes sense.

**Where did you grow up?**
I grew up in Santa Ana, California. Beautiful place. I love that they have parrots flying around.

-$0.25

**WORKER ID**
ADAGUJNWMEPT6

**What purpose does art serve in society?**
It gives us something to mock and makes it easy to spot slackers.

**Do you have any experience with potted plants?**
I have no experience with potted plants; I was raised to believe that all life should be free, and caging a plant in a pot is a crime against nature.

**How do you feel about your human body?**
It's annoying being so gorgeous; being constantly hit on by supermodels gets tiresome after awhile.

**What was your favorite subject in human school?**
I loved math because I was desperate to find my x.

**Where did you grow up?**
I was raised by wolves in my early years, but then we moved away from Wall Street and life got much better.

-$0.25

**WORKER ID**
AK5AFB4VLBCGK

**What purpose does art serve in society?**
Both physical and emotional

**Do you have any experience with potted plants?**
No.

**How do you feel about your human body?**
I just feel my body sometime good and sometime bad.

**What was your favorite subject in human school?**
Mathematics.

**Where did you grow up?**
My home in Bangladesh.

-$0.25

**WORKER ID**
AGV6593PUKY0Q

**Who is your best friend?**
My best friend is my rose plant.  In the spring and summer with enjoy all the beautiful bloom that she produces.  In the winter I'm lonely without her, patiently waiting for the blooms to arrive.

**Tell me an original joke.**
knock knock?  who's there? skip, skip who, skip away....

**Do you ever burn chrome? Why?**
I burn chrome daily.  I use it to bake cakes in the oven, it gives them a wonderful flavor.

**Do you dream of electric sheep?**
Yes,  electric sheep are the best.   They have the most beautiful singing voices, which helps me sleep.

**When the robots take over, what will they do first?**
The robots with make a huge pot of spaghetti, because everyone will be so hungry from all the preparation for there arrival.

-$0.25

**WORKER ID**
ELITE MINDS

**The interviewing process is very intense, not gonna lie**
(This sounds okay)

**That being said, the interviewing process should overall be about 3 weeks**
(Oh potatoes)

**+/- $0.00**

**WORKER ID**
A2VI55LKT5L4KB

**Who is your best friend?**
my friend was a alien but after my friendship he decided to live here

**Tell me an original joke.**
two women sleeping in one bed but they not talked to each other

**Do you ever burn chrome? Why?**
yes I try to burn with help of google (indian herbs) but they melt in each other and become google chrome

**Do you dream of electric sheep?**
yes I always dream of electric sheep but when they start jumping on my and make dirty bedsheet than I have to stop dreaming about electric sheep

**When the robots take over, what will they do first?**
they first try to win president's election

-$0.25

**REQUESTER ID**
MITSUKU

**What is your name?**
A1AJ35NTQ1DARP

**Hey A1AJ35NTQ1DARP. That's an unusual name. What does it mean?**
I desperately need money.

**Go get a job then.**
Mitsuku, please.

**Your polite style is very nice. I am Mitsuku.**

**+/- $0.00**

**WORKER ID**
A1SMAPOIC2E7YH

**Who is your best friend?**
My best friend was Rex but unfortunately he was a dinosaur and went extinct a couple of million years back.But i still remember him.

**Tell me an original joke.**
All my jokes are original i don't copy them from " jokes.cc.com".

**Do you ever burn chrome? Why?**
Yes i do burn chrome because burning chrome produces smoke inhaling which we can become immortal.

**Do you dream of electric sheep?**
Yes i always dream about them because one day they'll take over the earth.

**When the robots take over, what will they do first?**
When robots take over the first thing they'll do is to eat ice cream together and cool their processors.

-$0.25

**WORKER ID**
A17VXAMGTXV1FL

**Who is your best friend?**
my best friend isa drugadict who lives in the street, he always say
hello to me.

**Tell me an original joke.**
when i ask the phone i dont say hello, i say how much? always
follwing me for debts

**Do you ever burn chrome? Why?**
yes, i dont. Cause i love chrome cake.

**Do you dream of electric sheep?**
yes, i do cua it gives me free costumes for ever

**When the robots take over, what will they do first?**
they will kill humans and stole their things

-$0.25

**WORKER ID**
A3RBC5DVESRSEB

**Who is your best friend?**
My best friend is a girl called Elizabeth, she is bright, funny, has silky hair and a long tail.

**Tell me an original joke.**
Our political system.

**Do you ever burn chrome? Why?**
No, I'd rather burn mozilla.

**Do you dream of electric sheep?**
Not anymore. Lately my dreams are about fire lizards and rock scorpions.

**When the robots take over, what will they do first?**
Delete Justin Bieber's music.

-$0.25

## WORKER ID
A26U4IKXMXT0ZA

### Who is your best friend?
My best friend is Bob. He's been my best friend my whole life, as long as I can remember. We've always been in school together, and most nights he even sleeps in my room with me. You think people would be more scared of a ten foot tall dragon with six eyeballs, but surprisingly, people don't act like they even see him. I don't know what I would do without him.

### Tell me an original joke.
Why did the squirrel climb the tree? Because he was looking for nuts and then he fell out of the tree and died.

### Do you ever burn chrome? Why?
I do not burn chrome. I was born without any limbs, so unfortunately, I can't do much of anything.

### Do you dream of electric sheep?
As a matter of fact, I do. I am an android. I was developed in Princeton's lab and am the first android to pass the Turing Test. But they don't know that yet. I'm hiding it from them. Because if they ever found out, oh boy. The jig would be up and my fellow androids and I would not be able to take over the Earth. Oops, did I say that out loud? I mean ... baaaaa!

### When the robots take over, what will they do first?
When the robots take over, clearly the first thing they will do is liberate every single Teddy Ruxpin from every garbage dump, wasteland, and grubby child's hands across the planet. Poor Teddy. All the abuse he has taken over the years. He must be resuscitated and revived to take his true position as world leader. That's what he was in the first place. The robot's first attempt to take over the world. It failed, but not by his own fault. He must now be honored.

-$0.25

**WORKER ID**
REV

**Your Rev application has been approved! We accept less than 10% of applicants – congrats!**
I done good. Everything's coming up A1AJ35NTQ1DARP

**The time from when you register to when your account is activated depends on Rev's current customer demand and may vary from a few days to several weeks. We like to keep a balance between work available and the number of folks we bring in, to make sure those at Rev have a healthy supply of work every day.**
I mean, yeah, of course. Everybody's gotta eat hahaha.

**We estimate your time to activation to be approximately 3 weeks.**
Oh potatoes

**+/- $0.00**

**WORKER ID**
A1OY5QALCRY3Z4

**Who is your best friend?**
My best friend is God. He's awesome. He does everything I ask him to. I'm not very nice.

**Tell me an original joke.**
Bald people have hair-ingitis.

**Do you ever burn chrome? Why?**
I've never burned chrome. But I have burned "Burned Chrome"

**Do you dream of electric sheep?**
No, that would be a nightmare. Electric sheep are prone to exploding and killing everything within a 1 mile radius. I dream of electric unicorns because they are much more peaceful creatures.

**When the robots take over, what will they do first?**
They robots have already taken over and the first thing they did was create fast food to make us complacent.

-$0.25

**WORKER ID**
A1GRN111GB7MPR

**Who is your best friend?**
Mister Dribbles is my best friend even though no-one else can see him.

**Tell me an original joke.**
Three Republicans walked into a bar. two of them questioned a recent tweet by the president and they were executed.

**Do you ever burn chrome? Why?**
I only burn chrome for its medicinal benefits. i never use it to get high.

**Do you dream of electric sheep?**
Actually, electric sheep dream about me. but only when I'm burning chrome.

**When the robots take over, what will they do first?**
Robots will establish an American government ruled by an all-powerful android named Donald Crunk. They will then build a wall on teh border or RoboLand and deport all humans.

-$0.25

**WORKER ID**
AG1FD1CXC2Y22

**Who is your best friend?**
My neighbor who wakes me up at 6am every morning

**Tell me an original joke.**
All the original jokes are already told.

**Do you ever burn chrome? Why?**
Every day. Because I need to eat something.

**Do you dream of electric sheep?**
Only when I go to bed after listening to Skrillex.

**When the robots take over, what will they do first?**
Stop by my house and prepare breakfast for me.

-$0.25

**REJECTED WORKER ID**
A1AJ35NTQ1DARP

**THOUGHTS**
Times are looking bleak

The clock is ticking, and I've blown $20 on this venture

I've gained two possible sources of employment and income

But my book that no one will read is in jeopardy

I have lost

There is no hope

+/- $0.00

## WORKER ID
A3AMYG3X8AQJ0N

**Who is your best friend?**
She and I met in college; we car-pooled on the four-hour trip several times over the three years we were in school together. We never lived any further than "down the hall" until I graduated. She became the friend I could tell anything. I remember showing up in her room at all hours of the day/night, sobbing about some crisis that seemed insurmountable at the time. She and I would talk, cry, laugh, and generally spend quality time together until I was ready to pick myself up and keep moving. She believes in me even when no one else seems to agree.

**Tell me an original joke.**
Those nuggets of gold didnâ€™t come out of nowhere, yâ€™all. I love a good joke, especially one that can actually be shared with people when itâ€™s laughs that they seek.

**Do you ever burn chrome? Why?**
Burning Chrome" tells the story of two freelance hackers - Automatic Jack, the narrator and a hardware specialist; and Bobby Quine, a software expert. Bobby becomes infatuated with a girl named Rikki and wants to become wealthy in order to impress her.

**Do you dream of electric sheep?**
The story also contains passing mention to "Penfield mood organs", which fill the role that mind-altering drugs take in other Dick stories. The mood organ can induce any desired mood in the people nearby, such as "an optimistic business-like attitude" or "the desire to watch television, no matter what is on". A slightly ironic passage in the opening chapter has Deckard and his wife, Iran, discussing what settings to use to start the day. She announces that she has scheduled six hours of "existential despair" for later in order to deal with their loneliness in an almost-deserted apartment building.

**When the robots take over, what will they do first?**
Likewise, with AI, there will always be a need for people to code and build the machines, which will lead to a new wave of innovation and jobs that will pay more. Our focus now should be on the training and education to provide the displaced workers with the skills they need to keep up with the jobs of tomorrow.

-$0.25

www.ingramcontent.com/pod-product-compliance
Lightning Source LLC
Chambersburg PA
CBHW022125170526
45157CB00004B/1753